This book belongs to:

....

....

Editor: Carly Madden
Designer: Hannah Mason
Series Designer: Victoria Kimonidou
Editorial Director: Victoria Garrard
Art Director: Laura Roberts-Jensen

Copyright © QED Publishing 2015
First published in the UK in 2015
by QED Publishing
Part of The Quarto Group
The Old Brewery
6 Blundell Street
London N7 9BH
www.qed-publishing.co.uk

A catalogue record for this book is available from the British Library.

ISBN 978 1 78493 126 1

Printed in China

Stinky Jack and the Beanstalk

Written by Steve Smallman

Illustrated by Neil Price

Once upon a time there was a poor young boy called Jack.

He lived with his mum in a tumbledown house in the country.

Jack was so lazy he couldn't
be bothered to wash.

He began to **smell so bad** that his
mum made him sleep in the cowshed!

Daisy the cow
was not impressed.

One day, Jack's mum said,

"We've got no money left!
Go and sell Daisy and
make sure you get a
good price for her."

But Jack sold the cow
for just a handful of beans.

His mum was so cross that she
threw them out of the window.

Overnight, the beans grew into a huge beanstalk!

The next day, Mum sent Jack up the beanstalk to pick some beans.

Jack climbed higher and higher, until he came to...

...a giant's castle!

Jack was hungry,
so he knocked on the door
and asked a kind-looking
lady for some food.

She let Jack in and gave
him a slice of sausage.

After lunch the giant started
counting his money.

Jack had never seen so many gold coins.

Soon the giant fell asleep.

Jack crept out and picked up a
gold coin that had fallen on the floor.

He hurried back down the beanstalk
and gave it to his mum.

"Good boy," she gasped.
"This will pay to mend
our house."

"Now, please, Jack,
have a bath!"

But Jack shot back up the beanstalk.

Back at the castle, the giant's wife
let Jack back in. But then...

"FEE, FIE, FO, FUM!

I SMELL THE PONG OF AN ENGLISHMAN.

BE HE ALIVE OR BE HE DEAD,

I WISH HE WAS SOMEWHERE ELSE
INSTEAD!"
roared the giant.

"Nonsense," said his wife.
"It must be a blocked drain.
Now, eat your sausages."

"You're not coming into my lovely house until you're clean!" said Jack's mum.

Daisy wouldn't let him in the cowshed either!

So Jack had to sleep outside on a pile of leaves.

The next day, stiff and achy, Jack climbed back up the beanstalk.

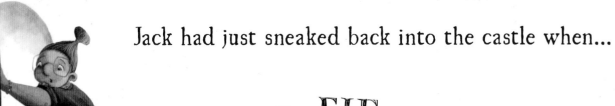

Jack had just sneaked back into the castle when...

"FEE, FIE, FO, FUM!

I SMELL THE PONG OF AN ENGLISHMAN.

BE HE ALIVE OR BE HE DEAD,

I WISH HE WAS SOMEWHERE ELSE INSTEAD!"

roared the giant.

"Nonsense, my dear," said his wife. "Perhaps you've trodden in something! Now, eat your sausages."

That evening, the giant fell asleep
listening to a magical, singing harp.

When Jack jumped out of his hiding
place the harp shouted,

"POOH, WHAT A PONG!"
and woke up the giant!

The giant grabbed Jack
in his huge hairy fist.

"Please don't eat me!"
cried Jack.

"I don't want to eat you!"
gasped the giant.

"I like having
visitors but only
ones who don't stink!

HAVE A BATH...
NOW!"

Jack ran to the bathroom.

The giant's wife
filled a tub with hot,
soapy water and at last,
Jack had a bath!
He even washed his hair.

He felt wonderful...
and he smelled delightful.

Jack enjoyed himself and decided
that washing was fun!

The giant invited Jack to stay for supper.

"I'm sorry
I took your gold,"
said Jack.
"I gave it to my mum to fix our
house and buy back our cow."

Blow Your Nose, Big Bad Wolf!

Don't Pick Your Nose, Pinocchio

"That's OK,"
said the giant kindly.
"Now, eat your sausage!"